Pier 21, harbourside, circa 1951. From the Kymlicka Collections of the Pier 21 Society

Pier 21:
STORIES FROM NEAR AND FAR

written by Anne Renaud

Lobster Press™

Dedicated to the staff, volunteers, newcomers, and military personnel, of years gone by, whose voices once filled the halls of Pier 21, and to the devoted individuals who keep its history alive, today.

I would like to extend my heartfelt gratitude to the following people who patiently and generously provided their time, knowledge, memories, photographs, and artifacts in support of this book. To my "first readers," Desmond Morton, Professor of History at McGill University and author of A Military History of Canada, and Mark McGowan, Principal of the University of St. Michael's College, University of Toronto. To Carrie-Ann Smith of the Pier 21 Society, and her colleagues, who steadfastly continue to preserve the history of Pier 21, on a daily basis. To Janet McNaugton, Sidney Coles, Joan Dodsworth Ware, Margaret Cameron, Josephine Mence, Philippe Grignon, Marylyn Emberley, Ausma Rowberry, Frank Weinfeld, Elisa Kleinas, Gerry Van Kessel and Tibor Lukacs who shared the rich pages of their family histories. To Garry Shutlak, of the Nova Scotia Archives, and Gail White, of the Westmount Public Library. To my editor, Meghan Nolan, and the staff at Lobster Press who weathered the process of bringing this project to fruition. Finally, to my childhood friend, Linda Malenfant, for being the best sounding board a writer could have.

Pier 21: Stories from Near and Far
Text © 2008 Anne Renaud
Illustrations © 2008 Aries Cheung

Published by Lobster Press™
1620 Sherbrooke Street West, Suites C & D
Montréal, Québec H3H 1C9
Tel. (514) 904-1100 • Fax (514) 904-1101
www.lobsterpress.com

Editors: Alison Fripp and Meghan Nolan
Editorial Assistant: Lindsay Cornish
Graphic Design: Olena Lytvyn
Production Manager: Tammy Desnoyers
Illustrations: Aries Cheung

Société
de développement
des entreprises
culturelles
Québec

We acknowledge the support of the government of Québec, tax credit for book publishing, administered by SODEC.

Library and Archives Canada Cataloguing in Publication

Renaud, Anne, 1957-
     Pier 21 : Stories from near and far / Anne Renaud ; illustrator, Aries Cheung.

ISBN 978-1-897073-70-4

     1. Ports of entry--Nova Scotia--Halifax--History--20th century--
Juvenile literature. 2. Canada--Emigration and immigration--History--
20th century--Juvenile literature. 3. Immigrants--Canada--History--20th
century--Juvenile literature. I. Cheung, Aries, 1960- II. Title.

JV7225.R46 2008   j325.71   C2007-905852-3

Kellogg's Corn Flakes is a registered trademark of Kellogg Company Corporation.

The views or opinions expressed in this book, and the context in which the images are used, do not necessarily reflect the views or policy of, nor imply approval or endorsement by, the United States Holocaust Memorial Museum.

Front cover *(from top, moving clockwise): Marylyn Rees's immigration card, Marylyn Emberley collection; Harbourside view of Pier 21, Author's collection; Immigration stamp, Marylyn Emberley collection; R.M.S. Mauritania, Author's collection; "Guest children" boarding the* S.S. Duchess of York, *bound for Halifax, Margaret Cameron collection; T.S.S. Athenia seating card, Janet McNaughton collection.*
Back cover: *Hat worn by immigration officials, Scotiabank Research Centre.*

Printed and bound in Singapore.

FROM 1928 TO 1971, a cavernous, shed-like building stood at the ready in Halifax Harbour to welcome more than one million newcomers to Canada and to send close to 500,000 Canadian service personnel off to battle during World War II.

Across its threshold came a tide of "home children" and "guest children," soldiers and war brides, refugees and displaced persons, carried to and from its doors by great ocean liners, military ships, and small sailing vessels.

This is a chronicle of Pier 21 and some of the people whose voices have resonated within its walls. It is a story of hope and courage in times of change and turmoil, and one of the many chapters in the history of Canada.

FIRST, THERE WAS PIER 2

Reproduced with the permission of the Minister of Public Works and Government Services Canada, and courtesy of Natural Resources Canada, 2007

ALREADY BY THE 1800s, Nova Scotia's Halifax Harbour 💼 boasted a long history of welcoming immigrants 🎩. Ships docked at a wharf located at the northern end of the city, where passengers disembarked.

In 1869, following Canada's first Immigration Act 🚂, an immigration office was established in Halifax, and by 1881, the Canadian government had declared the city an official port of entry. As the flow of hopeful newcomers increased, larger facilities were needed to accommodate their rising numbers.

Over the years, a pier and shed were built to receive the immigrants. It was called Pier 2.

HISTORY NOTES

💼 Halifax Harbour is the second largest natural harbour in the world. The First Nations people of Nova Scotia, the Mi'kmaq, populated the area known today as the Atlantic Provinces thousands of years before the arrival of European settlers. The Mi'kmaq called the harbour "Chebucto," meaning "biggest harbour."

🎩 Immigrants are people who move from one country, often their homeland, to permanently live in another country.

🚂 Canada passed its first Immigration Act, or law, in 1869, which dealt mainly with the safety of immigrant passengers aboard ships and the prevention of diseases from entering Canada. After the Act was passed, immigration offices were established in Halifax, Saint John, Quebec City, Montreal, Ottawa, Kingston, Toronto, and Hamilton, to receive newcomers to the country.

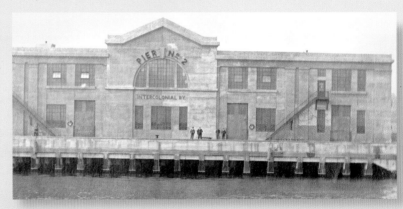

East end wall of Pier 2 shed, September 24, 1915 (Top). S.S. Andania and other vessels docked at Pier 2 (Bottom). A pier is a structure, which is built out from the shore into the water. It serves as a landing place where ships can dock. Library and Archives Canada (e008303436), and Nova Scotia Archives and Records Management

◀ *Mi'kmaq Women Selling Baskets, Halifax, circa 1845.* Library and Archives Canada (e000756682)

4

Anti-submarine net. Nova Scotia Archives and Records Management

Following the outbreak of World War I in 1914 🧳, Halifax was made battle ready. The city held frequent blackout practices, and submarine defence nets made of steel cable were strung across the entrance of the harbour for protection against German U-boats 🧢.

Halifax Harbour had become the busiest port in Canada. In addition to receiving immigrants, Pier 2 was the point of departure for thousands of servicemen en route to war-torn Europe, and was a most welcome sight for returning soldiers who had survived the battlefields.

But the morning of December 6, 1917, would bring great change to the city.

HISTORY NOTES

🧳 World War I was fought from 1914 to 1918. It involved many countries around the world including Canada, France, Britain, Russia, Italy, Belgium, Japan, and the United States, who fought against Austria, Hungary, Germany, Bulgaria, and Turkey. Over 60,000 Canadian soldiers were killed and 173,000 were wounded during World War I.

🧢 U-boat is short for *Unterseeboot* (under the sea boat), which means submarine in German. U-boats were feared because they launched weapons, called torpedoes, which could sink ships.

Immigrants arriving in early 20th century.

A Mighty Blast

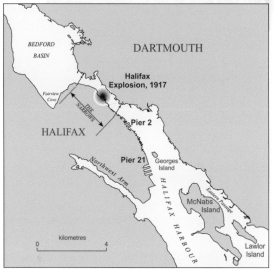

HISTORY NOTES

Merchant ships and troopships travelled "in convoy," which meant they were escorted by warships that protected them against German U-boats.

Map of Halifax Harbour. Reproduced with the permission of the Minister of Public Works and Government Services Canada, and courtesy of Natural Resources Canada, 2007

Made up of two parts, Halifax's inner harbour is called Bedford Basin. This is where ships gathered before sailing in convoy to Europe. The main harbour is where all types of naval and merchant ships were fuelled, repaired, and loaded or unloaded with military troops, supplies, and munitions. Connecting the two is a channel approximately 450 metres wide and one kilometre long, called the Narrows.

The *S.S. Imo* was among the many ships that were in the harbour on the morning of December 6. It was anchored in Bedford Basin and was preparing to leave for New York to pick up relief supplies destined for Belgium.

At approximately 8:15 a.m., as the *Imo* raised anchor and began to move through the Narrows on its way out to the open sea, the *S.S. Mont-Blanc*, a French munitions ship, entered the harbour and was making its way through the Narrows to join a convoy to Europe.

The *Mont-Blanc*'s cargo was not unusual for wartime, but it was extremely dangerous. While 35 tons of benzol, a highly flammable liquid, filled the barrels on its deck, more than 200 tons of TNT and 2,300 tons of picric acid, two chemicals used to manufacture explosives, were stored in its hold. The *Mont-Blanc* was a floating bomb.

Before long, the crew of both ships realised they were on a collision course. Just before 8:45 a.m., the *Imo* ripped through the bow of the *Mont-Blanc*, which sent sparks flying that ignited the benzol.

The crippled *Mont-Blanc* floated toward the northern area of Halifax, as columns of black smoke billowed 100 metres in the air. Unaware of the imminent danger, adults and children made their way down to the waterfront, while others stood at their windows for a better look at the burning ship.

Just before 9:05 a.m., the most destructive man-made explosion in Canadian history occurred.

Norwegian steamship Imo *beached on Dartmouth shore after the explosion.*
Nova Scotia Archives and Records Management

THE NET CIRCULATION OF THE GLOBE DURING NOVEM-BER, 1917, WAS 2,210,962. A DAILY AVERAGE OF 85,037

The Globe.

VOL. LXXIV. NUMBER 21,184. TORONTO, FRIDAY, DECEMBER 7, 1917—TWENTY PAGES. PRICE TWO CENTS.

THE WEATHER : Probabilities — Fair and cold.

HALIFAX DEAD MAY BE 2,000

HALIFAX, N.S., Dec. 6—Chief of Police Hanrahan to-night estimates that the dead from the explosion on a munition ship and subsequent fire, destroying a large section of the north end of the city, may reach two thousand. Another estimate says over two thousand. Twenty-five teams loaded with bodies have arrived at one of the morgues.

Over 2,000 people died and 9,000 were injured as a result of the explosion. The Globe, December 7, 1917.
Reprinted with permission from The Globe and Mail

Roome Street School. Eighty-eight students of Richmond School, Roome Street, Halifax, were killed in the explosion. Two children were in the school and eighty-six were either at home, or on their way to school. Nova Scotia Archives and Records Management

HISTORY NOTES

The blast that shattered the city of Halifax on December 6, 1917, was the most devastating man-made explosion before the United States dropped the atom bomb on Japan in 1945.

Following the explosion of 1917, the city of Boston and the state of Massachusetts sent doctors, nurses, equipment, and supplies to Halifax. To express their gratitude, every November since 1971, citizens of Nova Scotia select an evergreen from their forests, cut it down, and load it onto a ship in Halifax Harbour, destined for Boston. Upon its arrival, the tree takes centre stage at the annual Christmas tree lighting ceremony on the Boston Common.

In the wake of the massive blast, the entire north end of the city was levelled, railway cars were tossed around like toys, and windows more than 50 kilometres away shattered. Of Halifax's 60,000 residents, over 20,000 people were left without proper housing.

The immigration facilities at Pier 2 were badly damaged. Makeshift buildings were set up to greet newcomers following the devastating blast. By the time World War I ended in 1918, these people consisted mainly of Europeans fleeing their ravaged countries.

Because new and larger facilities were greatly needed, city officials looked to the south end of Halifax for a possible solution. There, an expansive waterfront provided the necessary space to receive the growing bulk of the ocean liners and their increasing number of passengers. The construction of a new immigration shed began, and on March 8, 1928, these facilities were officially opened.

And so began the story of Pier 21.

Merry Christmas Boston

Christmas tree donated by the province of Nova Scotia, arriving in Boston.
Department of Parks & Recreation, Boston

PIER 21

PIER 21 was not one building, but rather two buildings connected by covered overhead walkways. While the bottom floor of Pier 21's main building was used to receive cargo, the top floor was occupied by the immigration offices, as well as a number of facilities. These included the detention quarters 🧳, the hospital, the quarantine area 🎩, the jail cells 🚂, and the vault, where valuables and confiscated food items were kept ⭕.

Behind Pier 21's main building sat another two-storey structure called the Immigration Annex, which housed services designed to meet practically all the immediate needs of immigrants upon their arrival in Canada. Between the two buildings lay railway tracks.

After disembarking from their ship, newcomers were first led into a large hall lined with rows of benches called the Assembly Room. Amidst the clamour of voices of dissimilar languages, the cries and laughter of children, and the shuffle of feet, people sat clutching papers and passports, babies, and handbags, anxiously awaiting the round of interviews to begin.

Newcomers then met with immigration officials, who looked over their medical certificates and passports to make sure that every person was in good health, and had the necessary documents to enter the country. If all was in order, it was then time to continue on to the Immigration Annex.

Hat worn by immigration officials. From the Scotiabank Research Centre

Newcomers were sometimes given "ditty bags," which contained such items as soap, a toothbrush, tobacco, a sewing kit, and a toy for a child. These bags sometimes included Kellogg's Corn Flakes, which was regularly mistaken for chicken feed because of the word "corn" on the box. The floor of Pier 21 was often covered in cereal because offended newcomers would empty the boxes, thinking they had been given animal food.
From the Pier 21 Musem ditty bag exhibit

○ HISTORY NOTES

🧳 **Detention quarters** were like dormitory rooms. People were put in these quarters for various reasons. Some newcomers lived there until they could find proper housing or employment.

🎩 **The quarantine area** is where people were kept for a period of time because they might be carrying diseases that could be spread to others.

🚂 **On rare occasions**, newcomers were put in jail cells, also called strong rooms, because it was discovered they had criminal records. Sometimes these people were deported, meaning they were refused entry into Canada and were sent back to their country.

⭕ **It was forbidden** to bring certain types of food into Canada in case they carried germs or insects that could cause diseases. These foods consisted mainly of meats and cheeses, which were taken from immigrants when they arrived, and destroyed.

Canadian Government Railways: Ocean Limited between Montreal, St. John, Halifax Intercolonial Railway of Canada. From Halifax's Pier 21, immigrants then travelled inland by train to their final destinations. Library and Archives Canada (C-137809)

Within the walls of the top floor of the Immigration Annex were the offices of volunteer organisations, such as the Red Cross and the Sisters of Service. It also contained other facilities, including a nursery, a dining room, as well as stores and a canteen, where food and groceries could be bought.

In addition, the Annex housed the baggage room, where luggage could be reclaimed after having been inspected for illegal items, like weapons and certain types of food. Newcomers could also exchange any money they had for Canadian dollars at the Foreign Exchange Bureau, then purchase their train tickets at the Canadian National Railway and Canadian Pacific Railway wickets, before boarding a train that would take them inland to their final destinations.

As all this activity unfolded, volunteers were on hand to help Pier 21 staff greet, direct, reassure, and care for the newcomers.

Volunteer interpreters helped people who only spoke the language of their country communicate with the immigration staff. Other volunteers assisted in locating lost luggage, handed out "ditty bags," and some even gave money to those who did not have enough for train tickets or food supplies. Representatives from religious and social organisations were also available, such as the Sisters of Service, who helped find housing and employment, while others distributed

Immigrants arrived with a variety of trunks and suitcases. From the Pier 21 Museum exhibit

religious literature, offered counselling, or visited immigrants in the detention quarters. Red Cross workers bathed, fed, and cared for babies in the nursery, which had a number of cribs and beds where mothers and children could rest. A few volunteer organisations also provided escorts who travelled with immigrants aboard the trains until they had safely reached their destination.

Every day of the week over the course of 43 years, Pier 21 staff and volunteers worked steadfastly, some dedicating most of their lives aiding newcomers as they stepped through the doors of Pier 21.

Sisters of Service helping newcomers. Pier 21 Society

1928-1938

During the first half of the 20th century, Canada's immigration policies mirrored the intolerant beliefs of many Canadians about certain people. Newcomers were qualified as "preferred" or "non-preferred," depending on their race and where they came from. Among the "preferred" were people from Britain and the United States, because they spoke English, and it was felt that they would adapt easily to Canada. People from the northern and central countries of Europe were also welcomed, because they were willing to become farmers. "Non-preferred" immigrants included Blacks, Asians, and Jews. Changes were later made to Canada's immigration policies to eliminate such discrimination.

The Great Depression began in October 1929, when many people lost the money they had invested in the stock market, and lasted until the beginning of World War II. During these years, companies and industries collapsed, making jobs difficult to find in Canada. Most people lived in poverty.

FROM THE TIME Pier 21 opened its doors, immigrants from a variety of countries, including Poland, Belgium, Yugoslavia, Romania, Italy, and Czechoslovakia continued to arrive through the port of Halifax. However, as in previous years, the majority of newcomers came from Britain. The Canadian government considered British citizens to be very desirable immigrants, and had designed a number of programs to encourage them to settle in Canada, particularly as farmers to develop the West. In addition to reduced passage fares, young British men received help in finding work on Canadian farms, while young British women were assisted in securing employment as maids, also called domestics.

While the beginning of the 20th century saw a surge in the number of European immigrants, the Great Depression soon contributed to reducing the flow of newcomers.

Aboard the ships, passengers usually travelled in first, second, and third class, depending on the cost of their ticket. When the dining room was not large enough to accommodate all the passengers in their class at mealtime, they would be assigned a sitting time. Janet McNaughton *collection*

T.S.S. "ATHENIA."
Anchor-Donaldson Line.
Seating Card for First Sitting.
Barbara McIvor
Table............... Seat No. 191
R.E.R. Ltd.

The S.S. Nieuw Amsterdam was the first ship to officially arrive at Pier 21. It carried 51 immigrants. Author's collection

The McIvor sisters worked as domestics. They were hired by families and lived in their homes to provide cooking, cleaning, childcare, or other similar services. Janet is at left, Barbara is at right, and Jean is seated. Janet McNaughton collection

In 1928, Hugh and Janet McIvor and their ten children lived in a two-room apartment in Scotland. They had no indoor bathroom, and often stole vegetables from farmers' fields to supplement their meals. Hoping to improve their family's living conditions, 17-year-old Jean and 18-year-old Barbara McIvor sailed for Canada aboard the *T.S.S. Athenia* to seek employment as domestics. "After reaching Halifax on March 11, we travelled by train for two more days," explains Barbara. "As few trains were heated at that time, we kept warm by a potbelly stove, which we also used to heat water for our tea. At night, we slept in our seats made of narrow slats of wood. Within days of our arrival in Toronto, Jean and I found work and began sending most of the money we earned home to Scotland. Our third sister Janet soon joined us, and by the end of 1929, our entire family was reunited in Canada."

Potbelly stove used in railroad depots and train cabooses. P. Latondress/The Cochrane Railway & Pioneer Museum, Cochrane, Ontario

By 1935, Pier 21 was witnessing an increase in the number of departures, as jobless immigrants, who were no longer able to support themselves, were deported, or chose to return to their homelands. Among the few arrivals to spill through the doors of Pier 21 at the end of the 1930s were "home children" . Shortly after their entrance into Canada, these children were sent to live with families to work. Boys usually helped on the farm, while girls helped with household chores. The children were to be given shelter, food, a small allowance, and the opportunity to attend school. Sadly, not all of them were treated kindly by their new families.

HISTORY NOTES

British children who were orphaned, or whose parents were too sick or too poor to raise them, were cared for in orphanages, or "homes," such as the Barnardo Homes and the Middlemore Homes. These children became known as "home children." From the 1860s until the end of the 1930s, over 100,000 British "home children" were sent to Canada in the hope that they would have a better life.

Sidney Coles was placed in the Middlemore Home in Birmingham, England, after his family was evicted from their home. Three of Sidney's sisters were adopted outside the family, with an aunt adopting his youngest sister. Fourteen-year-old Sidney sailed to Canada on May 6, 1932, aboard the *S.S. Newfoundland*. "From Halifax, I travelled by train to Fredericton, New Brunswick, where I was first sent to work as a farmhand for the Blakes," says Sidney. "When mealtime came, I was not allowed to eat with them in the dining room, but had to eat alone in the kitchen. My next job was with the Hawkins, where I was treated just like family. During the war, I joined the Royal Canadian Air Force and I worked as an instrument technician. After the war, I married and had two children. Over the years, I returned to England to visit with my sisters and still remain in contact with them to this day."

Sidney Coles and three of his four sisters near their home in Rugby, England. Sidney Coles collection

Wooden wheelbarrow used on a farm.

During the war years, hundreds of thousands of Canadian servicemen and women left their loved ones behind to fight on the battlefields of Europe. Over 44,000 of them would lose their lives and would never see Canada again. Library and Archives Canada (PA-114799)

WORLD WAR II

🚢 When Canada entered into World War II on September 10, 1939, to help Britain fight the Nazis 💼, 🧢, Halifax was once again made battle ready 🚂.

Although immigration traffic had shrunk because of the war, Pier 21 remained active. Now under the jurisdiction of the Department of National Defence, a continuous stream of departing Canadian troops flowed from its structure. Luxury liners like the *R.M.S. Aquitania*, the *R.M.S. Queen Elizabeth*, and the *R.M.S. Queen Mary* were quickly converted into much-needed troopships. Stripped of all their fineries, the liners were repainted "ocean grey" for camouflage and were outfitted with sleeping bunks, which allowed them to carry thousands of soldiers at a time.

▲ As it travelled on its way to Canada with more than 1,400 passengers and crew, the T.S.S. Athenia *became the first British passenger ship torpedoed by a German U-boat in World War II. More than 100 people died when the ship sank.* Author's collection

German U-boat sailors surrendering to Royal Canadian ▶ Navy. Nova Scotia Archives and Records Management

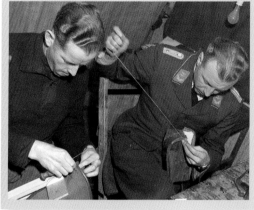

JEWS NOT ALLOWED

Jewish people were not always welcomed. Signs such as this one were posted in some Canadian neighbourhoods, at the entrance of sporting clubs, swimming pools, and other areas, in the 1930s and 1940s.
Canadian Jewish Congress Charities Committee National Archives

German prisoners of war mending clothing at Camp 44. Library and Archives Canada (PA-163785)

Group portrait of Jewish refugee children aboard the St. Louis. Despite their plight in Hitler's Europe, Canada accepted few Jewish refugees, before and during World War II.
USHMM, courtesy of Don Altman

As in World War I, troopships, merchant ships 🧳, and warships gathered once more in Bedford Basin before sailing in convoy.

Pier 21 was also kept busy with the arrival of returning soldiers, British evacuee children, prisoners of war, and refugees 🧢, 🚂. Ships came and went at all hours of the day and night, their departure and arrival times shrouded in secrecy 🛟.

HISTORY NOTES

🧳 Canadian merchant marine ships played a crucial role during the war. They carried food, weapons, and raw materials that Britain so desperately needed. With every Atlantic crossing, sailors faced the hazards of bad weather and deadly German U-boats.

🧢 Nearly 40,000 German and Italian soldiers and civilians were kept in prisoner-of-war camps located in Alberta, Ontario, Quebec, and New Brunswick, during World War II. Most of the camps had work programs. Some prisoners helped out on farms, while others constructed roads and buildings, or performed logging tasks, such as cutting down trees.

🚂 Refugees are people who flee their country because of war or the fear of being mistreated or tortured. On May 13, 1939, the ocean liner *S.S. St. Louis* sailed from Hamburg, Germany, for Havana, Cuba, with more than 900 Jewish refugees who were fleeing the Nazis and hoped to eventually find safe haven in the United States. Although they all had proper immigration papers, only a few passengers were allowed to disembark when the *St. Louis* docked in Havana Harbour on May 27. Jewish organisations negotiated with a number of countries, including the United States and Canada, to admit the refugees, but the countries refused. Finally, in June, Belgium, Holland, France, and England agreed to open their doors to them. However, by the end of 1940, the Nazis had invaded the first three of these countries, and most of the refugees died in Nazi prison camps.

🛟 At the beginning of World War II, top-secret shipments of Britain's gold and securities were sent to Canada for safekeeping, under the code name "Operation Fish." Unsuspecting dock-workers in Halifax unloaded the crates that were then placed aboard trains for Quebec and Ontario. Part of the precious cargo was stored in a vault located three storeys beneath Montreal's Sun Life Assurance Company building.

THE HALIFAX MAIL

373rd
Day Of The War
Against Barbarism

"What Stands If Freedom Fall?---Who Dies If England Lives?"

HALIFAX, CANADA, MONDAY, SEPTEMBER 9, 1940

AIR ATTACKS ON LONDON INCREASE

Who Dies If England Li...

HALIFAX, CANADA, MONDAY, SEPTEMBER 9, 1940

The Halifax Mail, September 9, 1940.
Courtesy of the Halifax Herald Limited.

Margaret Ferguson, second from left, and other British ▶
"guest children" boarding the S.S. Duchess of York,
bound for Halifax. Margaret Cameron collection

GUEST CHILDREN

AS HITLER'S war machine advanced across Europe, England soon realised it too might be invaded. In the summer of 1940, German bombs fell on London. At night, the air raid sirens wailed and people scrambled into bomb shelters. Fearful for their children, many British families decided to send them to other countries for safekeeping. These countries included the United States, Australia, South Africa, and Canada.

Many children were sent to Canada through a program funded by the British government called CORB, which stood for Children's Overseas Reception Board 🧳. From all over Britain, children travelled to Liverpool, England, and Glasgow, Scotland, to board ships bound for Canada. The children were allowed to take whatever could fit into one suitcase, and wore name labels pinned to their jackets and sweaters for identification.

In July, 1940, the first ship carrying CORB children to Canada steamed across the Atlantic 🧢.

Aboard the ships, children were divided into groups and assigned to an adult who took care of them during their trip. They were given life jackets, which they had to carry with them at all times. They also practised lifeboat drills as a safety precaution.

○ HISTORY NOTES

🧳 **Over 7,000 British children were evacuated to Canada for safekeeping at the expense of their families, or through the CORB program. The children were called "guest children" because they were considered to be Canada's guests.**

🧢 **During the war, the Canadian Broadcast Corporation, in collaboration with the British Broadcast Corporation, presented a radio program called "Children Calling Home." The two-way radio broadcast allowed "guest children" in Canada to speak to their parents in Britain.**

Christmas 1941, in Canada.
Joan Gibbons, far left, and
brother Alan, second from
right, with relatives.
Joan Dodsworth Ware collection

A child's teddy bear. From Pier 21 "guest children" exhibit

Joan Gibbons was 12 years old and her brother Alan was 7 when they were sent to Canada through the CORB program. "My brother and I sailed aboard the *S.S. Hilary* from Liverpool, England, and arrived at Pier 21 on August 16, 1940. We then travelled by train to Toronto and from there we joined relatives in Kingston, Ontario, who would take care of us," explains Joan. "I had never seen people eating corn on the cob before coming to Canada. In my native England, at that time, corn was only used to feed cows. After the war, my brother and I were reunited with our parents in England." In 1953, Joan married a Royal Air Force pilot and she returned to Canada, this time to make a home for herself and her husband.

Most of the ships carrying British evacuee children also travelled in convoy. However, this did not prevent them from being targeted by the enemy. On the night of September 17, 1940, the *S.S. City of Benares* was steaming toward Halifax when suddenly there was a huge blast. A torpedo had hit the ship.

In the darkness, children and adults scrambled on the ship's deck to board the lifeboats, but the stormy weather made the lowering of the lifeboats difficult. As each one landed in the water, it flooded. Many children were swept out of the lifeboats and drowned. Those who managed to remain inside sat waist-deep in icy cold water waiting to be rescued. Hours ticked by before the Royal Navy ships arrived. By then, many of the children had died from the cold.

The sinking of the *City of Benares* brought an end to the CORB program. For many of Canada's "guest children," it would be five years before they sailed the Atlantic back to their parents and families.

Articles belonging to the "guest children."
From Pier 21 "guest children" exhibit

The S.S. City of Benares. Pier 21 Society

Middle right: Among the 406 passengers aboard the City of Benares *were 90 children being evacuated to Canada for safekeeping. Only 13 children survived the sinking of the ship.*
The Montreal Gazette, September 23, 1940. Courtesy of the Montreal Gazette ▲

BRAVE YOUNGSTERS SING AS SHIP SINKS

Children Seek to Cheer Up Adults While Heavy Seas Batter Lifeboats

BOY'S HEROISM IS TOLD

Welsh Lad of 1...

The day 11-year-old Josephine Robson left England for Canada was the very first time she saw her father cry. Travelling aboard the *S.S. Oronsay*, with her 9-year-old sister Dorothy and 7-year-old cousin David, Josephine was seasick for most of the trip. Upon their arrival in Halifax in mid-August 1940, the children boarded a train for Montreal, the city in which they would live for the next five years. "While in Canada, we experienced many new things, like Montreal's annual Christmas parade, eating maple syrup, and learning French," says Josephine. "Although we missed our parents, it was with great sadness that we left our Canadian families when World War II was over."

From left to right, Josephine Robson, her sister Dorothy, and her cousin David. ▶
Josephine Mence collection

WAR BRIDES

HISTORY NOTES

 "War bride" describes the thousands of young women who met and married Canadian servicemen stationed overseas during World War I and World War II. While most World War II war brides were from Britain, some came from other countries, including Holland, France, and Italy. Between 1942 and 1947, approximately 48,000 war brides and 22,000 children travelled to Canada aboard luxury liners converted into wartime troopships. A few Canadian servicewomen married British husbands, who were nicknamed "male war brides."

Philippe Paul Grignon and his wife, Barbara Tomlinson, on their wedding day. At that time, it was a tradition for young brides to carry a horseshoe made of silver paper for good luck. Philippe Grignon collection

DURING World War II, hundreds of thousands of Canadian servicemen were stationed in Britain.

Before long, chance meetings with British women at dances and social events, when the soldiers were on leave, led to romance and marriage .

War brides and their children en route to Canada, from England, 17 April 1944. Library and Archives Canada (PA-147114)

Soldier Prefers Battle's Peril To Duty Upon 'Diaper Special'

Special to The Star
Ottawa, Feb. 8—"A Maid and a Million Men" is just a sissy to the army officer who has to ride a British war bride train from Hali-

most more than a mere man can stand.

"Wow!" he ejaculated, "when I think back on it. I remember I had to lock myself in the men's

A Canadian train was nicknamed the "Diaper Special." This is because of the many war brides and their children it transported across the country. The Toronto Daily Star, February 8, 1946. Courtesy - Torstar Syndication Services

Philippe Paul Grignon was one of the many Canadian soldiers aboard the *S.S. Batory*, which sailed from Pier 21 in March 1942. "My first taste of wartime Britain was a long train trip overnight with all the blinds drawn because of the blackout rules to prevent enemy planes from spotting us," explains Philippe. "As a radar operator and air gunner with the Royal Canadian Air Force, I was first assigned to air-sea rescue over the North Sea. One of our missions involved locating a small boat of Norwegians who were trying to escape from the Nazi invasion of their country, and bringing them to safety. It was while I was on leave in London in September of 1942 that I met Barbara Tomlinson. We married in Wembley, on May 29, 1944." Barbara sailed on the *R.M.S. Aquitania*, with her husband Philippe when he returned to Canada in February 1945. The couple settled in Toronto, Ontario, where they raised their two children

Military headquarters in London set up the Canadian Wives Bureau to register war brides and to assign them transportation to Canada. The Bureau cautioned war brides to be ready at a moment's notice. Letters informing them of their departure dates often arrived only days before they sailed, which left them little time to prepare for their trips. For the women who chose to follow their hearts to Canada, the possibility of never again seeing their families and friends was very real. This made for many heart-wrenching farewells.

Most of the war brides remained in Canada, though not all. Some, who lived in remote rural areas, were unable to adapt to the rugged living conditions of their adopted country. Others chose to return to their homelands because of overwhelming homesickness.

During the war, certain foods and other items were rationed, meaning that people could only have a limited quantity. This was to allow for supplies to be shared fairly among all people in Canada, as well as with Canadian soldiers overseas, and with Britain. The Gazette / Library and Archives Canada (PA-108300)

In June 2005, Canada Post issued a commemorative envelope to honour the thousands of young women who married Canadian servicemen and followed them to Canada to build a new life. © Canada Post Corporation (2005). Reproduced with permission

Dinner menu from the R.M.S. Scythia. Aboard ship, war brides and their children enjoyed food items they had not eaten for years, such as fruit and white bread, because of shortages in worn-torn Europe. Marylyn Emberley collection

▼

R.M.S. "SCYTHIA"   25th March, 1946

Diner d'Adieu

MENU

Petite Marmite

Poached Salmon—Sauce Hollandaise

Roast Turkey—Royale

French Beans   Braised Celery

Boiled and Browned Potatoes

Plum Pudding—Brandy Sauce

Ice Cream

Dessert   Coffee

◄ *War brides and their children were not considered "immigrants," because war brides were married to Canadians. This is why Marylyn's immigration card reads "non-immigrant."* Marylyn Emberley collection

Marylyn Rees's parents met at a Valentine's Day dance in 1941 in Titchfield, England. Peter Rees, a Newfoundlander, was working as a mechanic with England's Royal Air Force. Betty Speedy, a native of Southampton, England, was also with the Royal Air Force, and worked at sending and receiving messages on a Teletype machine. When they married, they spent only two days together before they had to return to their respective units. "I was born in June 1942," says Marylyn. "After the war, my mother and I sailed from Liverpool aboard the *R.M.S. Scythia* to rejoin my father, who had been released from military service and was now back in Newfoundland. We shared a cabin with other war brides and children, and arrived at Pier 21 on March 26, 1946. The war left me with a life-long fear of loud noises, because of the bombings."

The belief of a Communist state is that all property is shared equally among its people, as the government sees fit. The hope is that this will lead to a country where everyone is equal, and where citizens are neither very rich nor very poor. However, historically, this has led Communist governments to tightly control the lives of their citizens. Some of these governments have even used force against their own people to maintain this control.

A displaced person is a refugee. After the war, hundreds of thousands of people were unable to return to their homes and communities because they were destroyed by war or occupied by others. Camps for displaced persons were set up in countries across Europe, including Germany, France, Italy, and Belgium to house the refugees and provide them with food, clothing, and medical care. Some refugees remained in the camps for several years before they could resettle in other countries.

IN THE LAST MONTHS of World War II, Russian troops freed many countries from Nazi rule. Among these were Yugoslavia, the Ukraine, Poland, Hungary, Czechoslovakia, and the Baltic countries. However, following the end of the war, the Russian Communists remained and took over the governments of these countries. Their policies were oppressive and many citizens longed for their former independence and the homelands they once knew. As a result, thousands of displaced persons crossed the ocean in search of freedom.

The Levalds in April 1948, in Sillenbuch, Germany. This was the last camp for displaced persons that Ausma and her family lived in before immigrating to Canada. Ausma Rowberry collection

Ausma Levalds with two of her Canadian gifts. The doll with a bonnet and the silver locket were given to her when she arrived at Pier 21. Ausma Rowberry collection

In December 1944, Ausma Levalds and her family fled from Latvia on a cattle boat. The Levalds travelled to Poland and took refuge wherever they could until camps for displaced persons were set up after the war ended. From then on, the family lived for three years in camps until they made their way to Canada. It was with great bewilderment that Ausma disembarked at Pier 21 on February 10, 1949. The 8-year-old had no sooner stepped off the ship with her mother and sister than a sign with the number 50,000 was hung around her neck. Ausma was then presented with a doll, a silver locket, a Bible, and a "Birds of Canada" book. Why all the commotion? "Of the 1,200 passengers who sailed with me aboard the *S.S. Samaria*, I had been selected as the 50,000th displaced person welcomed into Canada," explains Ausma. "Shortly after our arrival, my sister, Rasma, my mother, and I joined my father and brother, Ilmars, who had immigrated to Canada nine months earlier to work on farms. Once united, our family settled in New Hamburg, Ontario."

Among the sailing vessels that carried newcomers to Canada were small, unseaworthy boats, overflowing with refugees from the Baltic countries of Estonia, Latvia, and Lithuania. With little more than the clothes they were wearing, many refugees arrived exhausted and starving, aboard crafts such as the *Capry*, the *Sarabande*, and the *Walnut*, which was designed to hold no more than 40 passengers, but counted 347 when it arrived in Halifax. Despite not having any proper immigration papers, almost all of these refugees were allowed to remain in Canada.

Perhaps ashamed for having done so little before and during World War II, Canada now opened its doors to Jewish refugees, including over 1,000 orphans through its War Orphans Project. The orphans were under the sponsorship of the Canadian Jewish Congress, which was responsible for making the necessary arrangements for their adoption by Canadian Jewish families. Between 1947 and 1949, a total of 1,123 orphans who had survived the Holocaust found new homes in Canada.

▲ *The more prosperous immigrants arrived with quantities of luggage, trunks, and crates. Others, particularly the refugees who entered Canada after World War II ended, arrived with only one tattered suitcase, and in some cases, with nothing more than the clothes they were wearing.* Canadian Jewish Congress Charities Committee National Archives

◄ *Photo of Joe Dziubak and other Jewish war orphans who survived the Holocaust. Joe is writing "Where are our parents, you murderers?" Only after the war did many orphans realize how few of their parents and family members were still alive.* Vancouver Holocaust Education Centre, Robbie Waisman collection

Frank Weinfeld at age 16, in France. Frank Weinfeld collection

Shortly after Frank Weinfeld's father was taken away to a Nazi concentration camp in 1944, his mother was imprisoned in the Budapest "ghetto," the enclosed area within the city where Jewish people were forced to live. Fourteen-year-old Frank never saw his father again. "After obtaining false identification papers, I survived the war in my native Hungary by selling cigarettes on the black market," explains Frank. "After the war, I made my way across Europe to France, where I met a representative from the Canadian Jewish Congress. I was granted a Canadian visa and sailed aboard the *R.M.S. Aquitania* from Southampton, England, with little more than the clothes on my back. I arrived in Halifax on October 26, 1947, and boarded a train for Winnipeg, where I settled, later married, and raised two children. In 1959, my mother left Hungary and joined me in Winnipeg, where she lived out the remainder of her life."

HISTORY NOTES

In 1866, a quarantine station was set up on Lawlor Island, which is located in the southeastern portion of Halifax Harbour. Its purpose was to care for sick immigrants whose illnesses could be transmitted to others. This, in turn, prevented the spread of diseases to the mainland. Over the years, vaccine programs and improved health measures were developed, which reduced the number of sick newcomers, and the need for the quarantine station. As a result, the station officially closed in 1938.

Elisa Bellissimo, at left, with her mother and her two brothers. Elisa Kleinas collection

Nine-year-old Elisa Bellissimo had not seen her father for four years when she arrived in Toronto in 1953. "My father had left our small Italian village in 1949 for Canada, to find work. For four years, he saved his money until he had enough for my mother, my two brothers, and me to join him," explains Elisa. "My family sailed to Canada aboard the *S.S. Conte Biancamano* on April 30, 1953. When I opened the bathroom door in our ship's cabin, I was in awe. It was the very first time I was seeing an indoor toilet and bathtub. Our home in Italy did not have any running water, and my family used chamber pots as toilets. I was even a little scared by the noise the toilet made when it was flushed."

Enamel chamber pot like the one used by Elisa Bellisimo's family. Author's collection

From 1947 onward, newcomers from other war-torn countries of Europe also crowded the halls of Pier 21. Many Dutch citizens came to Canada to establish farms, as large portions of Holland's agricultural land had been flooded during the war. Because their government forbade them from taking much of their money when they left their country, Dutch immigrants sailed to Canada with as many of their possessions as possible. Their large wooden crates surprised many Pier 21 officials because they contained a variety of household items, including, on one occasion, a kitchen sink.

New arrivals in Halifax also included Greek, Portuguese, German, and Italian immigrants, many of whom found employment as labourers in the mining, forestry, railway, and construction industries.

Before long, Pier 21 would also open its doors to nearly 20,000 Hungarians refugees.

On August 30, 1940, the S.S. Volendam was torpedoed by Nazis while carrying "guest children" to Canada. Although the ship was badly damaged, it did not sink, and all the children survived. Author's collection ▶

Gerry Van Kessel, at far right, and his family. Gerry Van Kessel collection

In 1951, 6-year-old Gerry Van Kessel and his family boarded the *S.S. Volendam* in Holland for Canada. "Upon our arrival in Halifax on February 22, medical staff discovered that two of my younger brothers had the mumps," says Gerry. "My family was put in quarantine at Pier 21 for three weeks until my brothers were better. It was there that I celebrated my 7th birthday on March 6, before my family and I were able to travel on to Ontario."

THE HUNGARIAN REVOLUTION AND THE 56ERS

ON OCTOBER 23, 1956, a group of Hungarian students and workers in the capital city of Budapest began to protest against the Communist government. Within days, thousands more Hungarian citizens joined them, and by October 28, there was a call for a countrywide general strike.

The Communist government sent in tanks and troops to restore order. They far outnumbered the Hungarian people and on November 4, after days of valiant fighting, the Revolution was defeated. In the aftermath, hundreds of Hungarians were imprisoned or killed. Over 200,000 people fled to Austria and Yugoslavia, and from there travelled to other parts of the world in search of a new country.

A burned-out tank in Budapest during the Hungarian Revolution. Tibor Lukacs collection

From 1956 to 1957, refugees from the Hungarian Revolution began to arrive in Canada, most of whom settled in Ontario. Known as "the 56ers," more than half of the nearly 40,000 Hungarians who made their way to Canadian shores came through Pier 21.

In 2006, Canada Post issued this envelope for the 50th anniversary of the arrival of nearly 40,000 Hungarian refugees to Canada. It bears the image of the Freedom Monument, which was erected for the 10th anniversary of the arrival of the "56ers" in Wells Hill Park on the shores of Lake Ontario. © Canada Post Corporation {2006}. Reproduced with permission

Tibor Lukacs, second from left, and his family, ready to depart for Canada. Tibor Lukacs collection

Two months following the defeat of the Hungarian Revolution, 11-year-old Tibor Lukacs and his family escaped from their homeland. "By the light of a full moon, we fled on foot on the night of January 18, 1957," explains Tibor. "To avoid capture by Communist soldiers, my parents, my two sisters, and I wrapped ourselves in white sheets, over our winter coats, so we would not be seen against the snowy backdrop of fields and highways. By early morning, we had crossed the Austrian border to safety and freedom. After living in a number of refugee camps for almost two years, my family and I eventually arrived in Canada by airplane in September 1958. For the following five-and-a-half months, we lived in Pier 21's detention quarters, while staff and volunteers helped us settle in our new country. My father was sad that we would have to celebrate our first Canadian Christmas without a tree, so he cut down a small evergreen in a nearby park and smuggled it under his coat back to his room. My family then decorated the tree with pieces of tinfoil and coloured paper, which cheered us up. We later settled in Toronto."

1960-1971

In 1959, Fidel Castro and his rebels toppled the Cuban government and established a Communist government in that country. Many Cubans, who did not want to live under Communist rule, left their homeland.

Young Greek girl arriving at Union Station, Toronto, Ontario, with 300 Greek and Italian immigrants after a stormy Atlantic crossing to Halifax, aboard Olympia. Library and Archives Canada (PA-122566)

The Globe and Mail, Saturday, August 31, 1968. Reprinted with permission from The Globe and Mail ▶

IN THE EARLY 1960s, mainly Greek and Italian immigrants continued to arrive at Pier 21. Its detention quarters also housed groups of Cuban refugees who, after arriving by plane in Gander, Newfoundland, travelled to Pier 21 to wait for their visas before continuing on their journey to the United States.

From August 1968 until early 1969, Pier 21 also saw the arrival of thousands of Czechoslovakian immigrants. Beginning in January 1968, under a new government that exercised less control over its citizens, Czechs had briefly had a taste of freedom. But in August 1968, Russian tanks thundered into Prague and crushed their hope of living in a more democratic society. As a result, thousands of Czech citizens fled their homeland. Of these, over 11,000 chose to rebuild their lives in Canada.

By this time, the number of immigrants arriving in Canada by large passenger ship was slowly dwindling as a result of the growing popularity of air travel. Immigration officers were now dividing their time between Pier 21 and the airport to meet newcomers. With more and more immigrants choosing the speedier and more affordable mode of transportation, it soon became clear that Pier 21 was no longer needed.

And so, on March 28, 1971, the immigration shed that had played host to hundreds of thousands of new Canadians for 43 years fell silent, as it officially closed its doors.

But this was not the end of Pier 21's story .

1,600 Czechs flee homeland daily UN group told

Canada's first Immigration Act	Halifax is recognized as an official port of entry	World War I	The Halifax Explosion on December 6	Official opening of Pier 21 on March 8	The Great Depression begins
1869	**1881**	**1914-1918**	**1917**	**1928**	**1929**

Reopening of Pier 21 on July 1, 1999. Pier 21 Society

The Nansen Medal. MCpl Serge Gouin, Rideau Hall

In 1986, the United Nations High Commissioner for Refugees awarded the Nansen Medal to Canada for the "remarkable achievement of individuals, families, voluntary agencies, community and religious organizations, as well as federal, provincial, and municipal authorities in helping refugees to integrate successfully into Canadian society and regain human dignity." This was the first time the award, which was created in 1954, was presented to an entire population, and not to an individual or organization.

PIER 21 REVISITED

FOR MORE THAN A DECADE LATER, Pier 21 served mainly as a training institute for merchant mariners and as a cargo-shipping warehouse.

In 1988, a group of local citizens formed the Pier 21 Society to breathe new life into the facility and to preserve Canada's last surviving ocean immigration shed as a place of memory. Pier 21 would now serve as a reminder of the crucial role of immigration in the building of Canada, and of the country's vital contributions during World War II.

In 1996, the Historic Sites and Monuments Board of Canada designated Pier 21 as a national historic site. Three years later, on Canada Day, July 1, 1999, Pier 21 reopened its doors as a museum and as a research centre.

In 2000, Canada Post issued a Pier 21 stamp as part of their Millennium Collection. © Canada Post Corporation {2000}. Reproduced with permission

World War II	The Canadian Citizenship Act takes effect on January 1	Pier 21 closes on March 28	Pier 21 Society is formed	Pier 21 is designated a National Historic Site	Pier 21 reopens on July 1, Canada Day
1939-1945	**1947**	**1971**	**1988**	**1996**	**1999**

Chief Justice Thibaudeau Rinfret presenting a citizenship certificate to Rt. Hon. W.L. Mackenzie King, Prime Minister of Canada, during the first citizenship ceremony to take place following the enactment of the Canadian Citizenship Act. Library and Archives Canada (PA-197418)

Today, looking out from the World War II Veteran's Deck on the top floor of Pier 21, visitors can see where the large net made of cables was strung up during the Second World War to prevent enemy submarines from entering the harbour. It is also here that descendants of immigrants, whose Canadian journey began at Pier 21, can obtain detailed information on the arrival of their ancestors.

Official citizenship ceremonies are held every year on Canada Day in the halls of the former immigration shed to welcome new immigrants to their adopted homeland 🧳, 🧢. The diversity of the people who crossed the threshold of Pier 21 mirrored the tumultuous times that spanned the 43 years of the immigration shed's existence. Every person had a story all their own, and each one has left an imprint on the fabric of our country.

A citizenship ceremony today.

HISTORY NOTES

🧳 Prior to 1947, Canadians were considered British subjects living in Canada, not Canadian citizens. On January 1, 1947, Canada became the first Commonwealth country to gain its own Citizenship Act. William Lyon Mackenzie King, who was Canada's Prime Minister at that time, received the first Canadian citizenship certificate when the ceremony was held in Ottawa.

🧢 The Commonwealth is a group of countries, including Canada, India, Australia, and New Zealand, that were once governed by Britain and part of the British Empire. Queen Elizabeth II is the Head of the Commonwealth, and is recognized by these countries as their symbolic ruler.